Victoria and Albert Museum

German
wood
statuettes
1500–1800

Michael Baxandall

LONDON
HER MAJESTY'S
STATIONERY OFFICE
1967

Early in the 16th century the guilds and merchants of southern Germany, who for fifty years had been filling their churches with massive retable altars made by the late gothic wood-carvers, began to lose their taste for grand artistic gestures of this kind. There seems no simple explanation for the change in fashion; a decline in the burghers' own social confidence and even the fact that most churches now had quite enough retables already may have been just as important as the approaching crisis in German religious life. Whatever the reasons, the source of much of the livelihood of south German sculptors dried up, and other genres more in line with the new taste were anxiously tried out. These tended to be on a very small scale: sculptors trained in large-scale wood sculpture found themselves making portrait medals or small limestone reliefs, and they were not all very successful. The most effective development was in the art of the small statuette in wood, partly because this preserved most continuity with older skills and achievements.

The wood statuette offered the sculptor special opportunities. It was an intimate and comparatively cheap thing to buy, and could enlarge on preoccupations only hinted at in larger and more formal sculpture. In small works intended for the study or the cabinet it was acceptable to indulge an interest in, say, the physical nature of death and old age, or even a nostalgia for the art of the late middle ages. Their relation to the artist himself was intimate in a rather different sense. Where the Italian sculptor tended to work out his ideas by modelling in clay, the German often did so by cutting at wood, and in many of the best statuettes something of the informal and transitional character of the sketch survives. The very smallness of the figures brought the sculptor into close contact with the physical qualities of the wood he was using, and this was often fruitful. Typically the wood was boxwood, the finest and, with the rather coarser pearwood, the most frequently used material for the better class of statuette. Boxwood, which had long been imported into Northern Europe from the Mediterranean and the Black Sea for purposes of fine carving, is a very dense and evenly grained wood, and can be cut cleanly in all directions; its natural yellow colour darkens with age to a rich deep brown, and its surface reacts pleasantly to polishing and even to staining. It was in terms of these qualities and their exploitation that the wood statuette was first developed.

Veit Stoss of Nuremberg, who had once made for the German church of St. Mary at Cracow the largest of all the surviving retable altars, was one of the sculptors forced to adapt his skills to the new market for statuettes. In carving his Virgin and Child (Plate 1) he was in competition with the goldsmiths, who produced silver figures of the Virgin on the same scale in very large numbers. His resource was to use the elastic properties of boxwood to the limit and set his own virtuosity with swinging arcs of drapery against the glitter of the goldsmith's material, and in doing so he was playing on one of the commonplaces of the new humanism: the priority of human skill over any preciousness of the matter it exercises itself upon. The starting point for his design was a solemn and monumental 15th-century type of the Virgin holding the Child very high indeed to her left, each gazing seriously into the face of the other, but Stoss transformed the whole effect of this by turning both heads to grin straight at the beholder. To anyone used to the old type such immediacy was and still is almost shocking, or would be so in a life-sized figure; in a figure eight inches high the effect is instead artful and personal, and quite beyond the range of any of the Nuremberg goldsmiths of Stoss's time.

As the 16th century progressed the old religious themes were very soon joined by an Italianate range of subjects reflecting the new interest in classical antiquity (Plates 6, 7). In these secular figures the sculptor's skill and ability to charm could be displayed without any inhibitions at all, and by the later part of the century this concern with art as art, rather than as an instrument of piety, began to take a curious turn. An interest and a market developed in the art of the past, particularly in the work of the earlier 16th century, and many sculptors took advantage of this new fashion. The distinction between fake and pastiche often becomes very difficult to draw here. Some figures seem to have the intention of being deceptive and of passing as what they are not (Plates 8, 9), others only play with formal ideas drawn from earlier styles (Plate 10). But it is clear that the antiquarian awareness of the collectors and sculptors extended over a wide field, from Burgundian work of the early 15th century (Plates 8, 9) to native German work of the mid-16th century (Plate 11). The fashion found an institutional form in the Kunstkammer, the forerunner of the modern museum, and many of these sculptures were produced for such collections.

Though this strange retrospective episode in German sculpture was based on an interest in artists' styles, the preoccupation with carving pieces in an archaic manner had the effect of weakening the sculptor's concentration on the special possibilities of his medium, and during the 17th century its development was even more limited by an unsuitable kind of competition with the revived art of ivory carving. Ivory was a more expensive and now a more fashionable material for statuettes than any of the woods; even boxwood became a poor relation. The better talents naturally spent their time on the more profitable ivory, and most 17th-century boxwoods were produced either by inferior carvers or as a sideline from workshops conditioned by ivory carving styles (Plates 12, 13). Instead of using all the qualities of their wood, sculptors now tended to confuse the forms they carved in boxwood with those most conveniently carved in ivory, and wood statuettes were often committed to an alien level of gloss and fretted detail (Plates 22, 23). For this reason many of the more interesting wood statuettes of the later 17th and early 18th centuries tend to be a little freakish—survivals of the old retrospective interest (Plates 16, 17), objects made without the market in mind (Plates 18, 19), or figures made in regions where the art of ivory carving was less dominant (Plates 20, 21). By the early 18th century the statuettes were also suffering through competition from the new porcelain figures.

Displaced more and more from its politer role by ivory and porcelain, the wood statuette escaped into a last bohemian fling. As long as the carver had been emulating the effects of a material very unlike his own, wooden statuettes had been isolated from the main stream of wood sculpture. With the genre socially in eclipse the statuettes now assimilated themselves increasingly to the sculptor's informal sketch model, and by doing so recovered contact with the most vital processes of wood-carving, though it was a contact of a new kind. For the first time there is in the 18th century a continuous range from the sketch of a first idea to a virtuoso statuette; neither entirely excluded the function of the other. Paul Egell's model for a Jesuit Saint (Plates 24, 25) was a sketch for a large altar- or wall-figure, yet it was preserved and mounted after its first purpose was achieved or abandoned. The Franconian Huntsman (Plates 26, 27) probably started off as a model for stone garden-

4

sculpture and may well have been worked up and lacquered only after taking somebody's fancy. Just as Veit Stoss's Virgin and Child had drawn its vocabulary and force from its relationship with monumental sculpture, Dietz's Goatherd (Plate 28), because it was intended first as a guide to the carving of garden sculpture, did the same.

This last flowering was short. The coquettish lounging of the Huntsman represents very exactly what Winckelmann disliked about the rococo conception of the figure, and by the last quarter of the century Winckelmann had effectively crippled many people's receptivity to this sort of thing. German sculptors were now learning to carve nobly in marble and, by corollary, sketch soberly in clay. Once they had done so the period of the wood statuette was over.

1   VIRGIN AND CHILD. Boxwood with traces of gilding. By
     Veit Stoss (d. 1533). Nuremberg; about 1520. Plates
     1–3.
     H. 8 in. (without base) (20·32 cm.). 646–1893.
     The figure is the only secure example of a statuette by
     Stoss, though small-scale sculpture appears to have
     made up a large and prized part of his later work (cf.
     Johann Neudörfer, *Nachrichten von Künstlern und
     Werkleuten* [1547], ed. G. Lochner, 1875, p. 84). The
     ascription was first made by Voss and has not been
     disputed. There are traces of a narrow gilt band run-
     ning round the edge of the cloak and head veil, and
     this is probably original.

     Voss, in *Repertorium für Kuntswissenschaft*, XXXI,
     1908, p. 258; Lossnitzer, *Veit Stoss*, 1912, p. 128;
     Daun, *Veit Stoss und seine Schule*, 1916, pp. 139–40;
     Lutze, in *Pantheon*, XIX, 1937, p. 188, and *Veit Stoss*,
     1938, p. 38; Th. Müller, in Thieme-Becker *Künstler-
     Lexikon*, XXXII, 1938; Stafski, in *Anzeiger des Ger-
     manischen Museum*, 1936–9, p. 132; Dettloff, *Wit
     Stosz*, I, 1961, pp. 161–2.

2   AN OLD WOMAN. Pearwood, partly pigmented. South
     German (?Nuremberg); about 1525. Plates 4, 5.
     H. 6¼ in. (15·88 cm.). 62–1865.
     This statuette, a version in bronze in the Bibliothèque
     Nationale in Paris, and a version in wood formerly in

the Paul Gerngross collection in Vienna were published by Planiscig as Paduan work in the style of
Riccio, together with a related group of bronze and
wood figures of the same subject. The figure is German, though attributions by Otto to Gregor Erhart and
by the Catalogue of the Exhibition *Augsburger Renais*
sance (1955) to the circle of Stephen Schwarz seem too
specific. The character of the Paris bronze points rather
to Nuremberg. The seat, lacking in the other figures,
seems to be 16th-century work.

Planiscig, *Andrea Riccio*, 1927, pp. 90–1; Otto, in
Schwäbische Heimat, V, 1954, p. 251; Städtische Kunstsammlungen Augsburg, *Ausstellung Augsburger Re*
naissance, 1955, pp. 78–9, No. 433.

3 VENUS. Pearwood. By an imitator of Conrat Meit.
German; second quarter of the 16th century. Plates 6, 7.
H. $9\frac{7}{8}$ in. (without base) (25·08 cm.). A.4–1956.
The figure has been described as *A Dancer* and also as
Lucretia but seems rather to be a *Venus* from a group
of the Judgement of Paris. Published by Winkler as
by Conrat Meit (d. 1550/51), it is one of a series of
hardwood statuettes attributed by Troescher and Bange
to a sculptor working around 1525 in Meit's shop or
under his influence. This sculptor consistently uses
Meit's types and formulas but is distinguished by a
softened handling of detail and facial expression. His
place of work has not been identified, and it is not
certain that he was contemporary with Meit. A group
of the *Judgement of Paris* by the same hand is in the
Germanisches Museum in Nuremberg.

Winkler, in *Jahrbuch der preussischen Kunstsammlun*
gen, XLV, 1924, p. 46; Troescher, *Conrat Meit von*

Worms, 1927, p. 50 and p. 72, note 106; Bange, *Die Kleinplastik der Deutschen Renaissance in Holz und Stein*, 1928, pp. 65–8; Braun, *Kleinplastik der Renaissance*, 1953, p. 5.

4 VIRGIN AND CHILD. Boxwood. South German; late 16th century. Plates 8, 9.

H. 4⅞ in. (12·58 cm.). A.534–1910. Salting Bequest.

A very similar group from the former Hohenzollern collection at Sigmaringen, now in the Städtischen Skulpturengalerie in Frankfurt (Inv. 903), is incised with the date 1417. It is suggested by Müller that both are 16th-century copies after early 15th-century Franco–Burgundian originals, and this suggestion is reinforced by the fringed shawl of the present statuette, evidently a reminiscence of the *Schöne Madonna* of Regensburg (1519). The consistency of the faking fails at the back of the group, and it is likely that the original, probably in stone, was on a much larger scale and modelled only at the front and sides.

Th. Müller, in *Festschrift für Erich Meyer*, 1958, p. 196, note 16, and in *Bayerische Akademie der Wissenschaften, Philosophisch-Historische Klasse, Sitzungsberichte 1961*, I, 1961, p. 14.

5 VIRGIN AND CHILD. Pearwood. Augsburg; about 1600. Plate 10.

H. 10½ in. (26·67 cm.). 28–1881.

The group derives from a Düreresque composition of the type of the engraving B.33. It is an example of a domestic religious image carved in the more moderate archaising style of the period round 1600. There is no attempt in the drapery to reproduce the manner of the early 16th century and it is distinct from such Kunst-kammer pieces as No. 4.

6   ADAM. Boxwood. Augsburg; about 1600. Plate 11.
H. 13$\frac{5}{8}$ in. (34·61 cm.). A.22–1951.
A replica in the late 16th-century taste of one of a pair of mid-15th-century pearwood statuettes of Adam and Eve, now in the Kunsthistorisches Museum in Vienna. The Vienna figures were attributed by Bange (*Kleinplastik der Deutschen Renaissance in Holz und Stein*, 1928, pp. 88–9) to the circle of the Nuremberg goldsmith Wenzel Jamnitzer and, more persuasively, by Vöge (*Jahrbuch der preussischen Kunstsammlungen*, LIII, 1932, p. 158) to Christoph Weiditz, a gold-smith and medallist who settled in Augsburg in 1532. There are similar Kunstkammer replicas of the Adam and Eve in the Kunstgewerbemuseum in Leipzig.

Th. Müller, *Münchner Jahrbuch der bildenden Kunst*, VIII, 1957, p. 122, note 2.

7   THE REPENTANT THIEF. Boxwood, lacquered. By Jörg Petle (1601–34). Augsburg; about 1625. Plate 12.
H. 10$\frac{3}{4}$ in. (27·3 cm.). W. 10$\frac{9}{16}$ in. (26·84 cm.).
A.26–1951. Given by Dr. W. L. Hildburgh.

7a THE UNREPENTANT THIEF. Boxwood, lacquered. By Jörg Petle (1601–34). Augsburg; about 1625. Plate 13.
H. 1 ft. $\frac{1}{2}$ in. (31·75 in.) W. 9 in. (22·86 cm.).
A.27–1951. Given by Dr. W. L. Hildburgh.
There are other and slightly varied versions of both Thieves in boxwood in the Musées Royaux d'Art et d'Histoire at Brussels, in gilt bronze in the Staatliche Museen at Berlin, and in bronze, together with a figure of Christ Crucified, in the Folkwang-Museum at

Essen. The attribution to Petle is due to Schädler; a suggestion by Theuerkauff that the Thieves are from an Italian or Italo–Flemish workshop is less persuasive. Neither figure shows any sign of having been attached to a cross.

Th. Müller and Schädler, *Georg Petel 1601–1634.* 1964, p. 24; Theuerkauff, in *Kunstchronik*, XVII, 1964, p. 205.

8 DIANA. Boxwood. By Leonhard Kern (1588–1663). German; second quarter of the 17th century. Plates 14, 15.
H. 8⅞ in. (22·54 cm.). A.1–1922.
The type and style are closely similar to a pearwood figure of Eve in the Herzog-Anton-Ulrich-Museum in Brunswick, signed by Kern, and the attribution has not been disputed. The Diana is one of a number of works by Kern, who was in Italy for some time between 1610 and 1620, in which the figure style is assimilated to that of German sculpture of the first half of the 16th century. None of Kern's statuettes is dated and no acceptable chronology has been worked out for his œuvre.

Sauerlandt, in *Belvedere*, V, 1924, p. 55; J. Müller, Thieme-Becker *Künstler-Lexikon*, XX, 1927, p. 182 (*s.v.* Kern); Fillitz, in *Jahrbuch der Kunsthistorischen Sammlungen in Wien*, 53 (XVII), 1957, p. 216.

9 DEATH. Limewood. Bavarian; second half of the 17th century. Plates 16, 17.
H. 11 in. (less base), (27·94 cm.). 299–1870.
This *memento mori* is one of a group of 17th century wood statuettes, published by Müller, reviving the

late medieval and renaissance small figures of Death.
A closely comparable figure in the Oberhausmuseum at
Passau is incised under its base with the date 1673. The
bow and the quiver are not original.

Berliner, *Katalog des Bayerischen Nationalmuseums,
XIII, 4, Bildwerke in Elfenbein,* 1926, p. 44; Th.
Müller, in *Zeitschrift des deutschen Vereins fur Kunst-
wissenschaft,* X, 1943, pp. 255–61.

10   MALE ACADEMY FIGURE (ADAM). South German;
about 1700. Plate 18.
H. 1 ft. 1⅞ in. (35 24 cm.). A. 14–1951.

10a FEMALE ACADEMY FIGURE (EVE). South German;
about 1700. Plate 19.
H. 1 ft. 1⅛ in. (33.54 cm). A.15–1951.
The modelling of these figures is highly schematic and
suggests, particularly in the torso of the female figure,
that they were carved after *Gliederpuppen* or lay-
figures. The degree of schematization is unusual in
lying somewhere between the functions of a proportion
figure and of an articulated lay-figure used for teaching
drawing (for which, see Meder, *Die Handzeichnung,*
1919, pp. 225 and 554–7). The arms and the hands on
the arms are separate and roughly attached, and may
well have been frequently reset.

11   COURAGE. Boxwood. Austrian; first quarter of the 18th
century. Plate 20.
H. 9 11/16 in. (without base). (24.62 cm.) A.1–1948.
Given by Dr. W. L. Hildburgh.

11a FEAR. Boxwood. Austrian; first quarter of the 18th
century. Plate 21.

H. 9 $\frac{11}{16}$ in. (without base). (24·62 cm.). A.2–1948. Given by Dr. W. L. Hildburgh.

The statuettes are probably by the same hand as a group of David and Goliath in Vienna (Schlosser, *Werke der Kleinplastik in der Skulpturensammlung des A. H. Kaiserhauses*, II, 1910, Plate XXX, 2); the attribution of the Vienna group to Josef Thaddäus Stammel by Schlosser and, much more tentatively, by Mayr (*J. Th. Stammel*, 1912, p. 30) is not very convincing, but this and the present statuettes are certainly Austrian work of the early 18th century. The two figures, leonine and hare-faced, are a physiognomic extension of earlier emblematic types: for the Aristotelian association of the hare with timidity, standard to the emblem-books, cf. Ripa, *Iconologia*, 1611, p. 515.

Burlington Magazine, XCVI, 1954, p. 329; H. D. Molesworth, *Baroque, Rococo and Neo-classic Sculpture*, Victoria and Albert Museum, Large Picture Book XI, 1954, p. viii.

12 ALEXANDER. Boxwood. Bavarian; early 18th century. Plate 22.
H. 1 ft. 1$\frac{1}{2}$ in. (34·29 cm.). 169–1864.

12a JULIUS CAESAR. Boxwood. Bavarian; early 18th century. Plate 23.
H. 1 ft. 1$\frac{1}{2}$ in. (34·29 cm.). 170–1864.

The relief on the base of the Alexander shows Deinocrates's project for the remodelling of Mount Athos in Alexander's image; that on the front of the base of the Julius Caesar the infancy of Romulus and Remus. These figures, together with a number of other small works in ivory and boxwood, have been attributed by Berliner to Matthias Loth, a name recorded in documents as that of an ivory carver active in Munich between 1705 and 1738. Neither the grouping nor the attribution to Loth seem very well-founded, but the style of the figures does point to an early 18th century Bavarian carver with a technique formed on ivory.

Berliner, in *Festschrift für Georg Habich*, 1928, pp. 104–11.

13 A JESUIT SAINT. Pearwood. By Paul Egell (1691–1752). Mannheim; about 1730. Plates 24, 25.
H. 9⅜ in. (without base) (23·81 cm.). A.5–1911.
This sketch is rightly attributed by Feulner to Paul Egell of Mannheim, though it is unusual among Egell's models in being wood rather than terracotta. The object held by the putto is a skull, and this identifies the figure as either St. Aloysius Gonzaga or St. Francis Borgia. A connection is possible with Egell's work for the Jesuit College (from 1730) or the Jesuit Church (from about 1750) at Mannheim, but the best analogies for the movement and drapery are in Egell's earlier work, particularly the Altar of the Immaculate Conception for the cathedral at Hildesheim (1729–31).

Feulner, in *Zeitschrift des Deutschen Vereins für Kunstwissenschaft*, I, 1934, p. 144.

14 A HUNTSMAN. Boxwood, lacquered. Würzburg; third quarter of the 18th century. Plates 26, 27.
H. 13 1/16 in. (33·18 cm.). A.38–1953. Bought under the Bequest of Capt. H. B. Murray.
This statuette seems to be a worked-up model for stone sculpture and may represent Actaeon or, possibly, Ganymede. The closest analogies for its style are from the Wolfgang Auwera/Peter Wagner workshop at Würzburg in the period 1750–65, particularly four

small figures of seasons formerly in the Dispensary of the Juliusspital at Würzburg (*Kunstdenkmäler des Königreichs Bayern*, III, xii, 1915, p. 532, fig. 411). The Viennese character of the head type and the relatively consequential musculature are consistent with the training of both Auwera (1708–56) and Wagner (1730–1809) at the Academy in Vienna. The figure is distinct from the plumper and more rustic rococo of Dietz (No. 15) and also from the neo-classical turn of Wagner's later work.

Burlington Magazine, XCVI, 1954, p. 329; H. D. Molesworth, *Baroque, Rococo, and Neo-classic Sculpture*, Victoria and Albert Museum, Large Picture Book XI, 1954, p. viii.

15 A GOATHERD. Limewood, lacquered. By Ferdinand Dietz (1708–1777). Franconia; third quarter of the 18th century. Plate 28.

H. 10⅞ in. (27·62 cm.). A.39–1953. Bought under the bequest of Capt. H. B. Murray.

The figure is a model for stone garden sculpture. It is characteristic of Dietz's work during the 1760's and 1770's for the gardens of the Prince-Bishops of Bamberg and Würzburg at Seehof and Veitshöchheim. There are a number of comparable wood models by Dietz, many of them pigmented, in the museums at Würzburg, Nuremberg and Munich (cf. *Münchner Jahrbuch der bildenden Kunst*, I, 1950, pp. 252–3, and V, 1954, p. 227; Schaffer, *Die Plastik des Ferdinand Tietz*, 1958, figs. 37–45).

Burlington Magazine, XCVII, 1955, p. 92. H. D. Molesworth, *Baroque, Rococo and Neo-classic Sculpture*, Victoria and Albert Museum, Large Picture Book XI, 1954, p. viii.

1 VEIT STOSS: Virgin and Child (Cat. no. 1)

2 VEIT STOSS: Virgin and Child (Cat. no. 1)

3　VEIT STOSS: Virgin and Child (Cat. no. 1)

4 SOUTH GERMAN: about 1525: An Old Woman (Cat. no. 2)

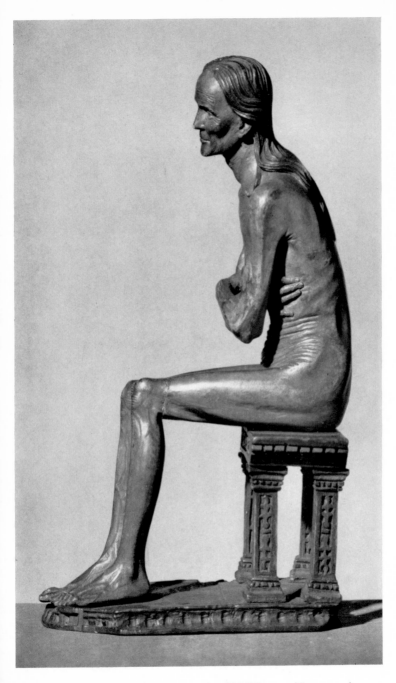

5   SOUTH GERMAN: about 1525: An Old Woman (Cat. no. 2)

6   GERMAN: SECOND QUARTER OF THE SIXTEENTH
CENTURY: Venus (Cat. no. 3)

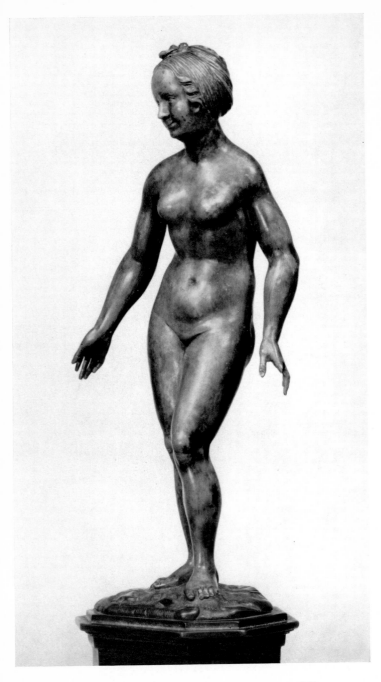

7   GERMAN: SECOND QUARTER OF THE SIXTEENTH
CENTURY: Venus (Cat. no. 3)

8 SOUTH GERMAN: LATE SIXTEENTH CENTURY: Virgin and
Child (Cat. no. 4)

9 SOUTH GERMAN: LATE SIXTEENTH CENTURY: Virgin and Child (Cat. no. 4)

10 AUGSBURG: about 1600: Virgin and Child
(Cat. no. 5)

11 AUGSBURG: about 1600: Adam (Cat. no. 6)

12 JÖRG PETLE: The Repentant Thief (Cat. no. 7)

13 JÖRG PETLE: The Unrepentant Thief (Cat. no. 7a)

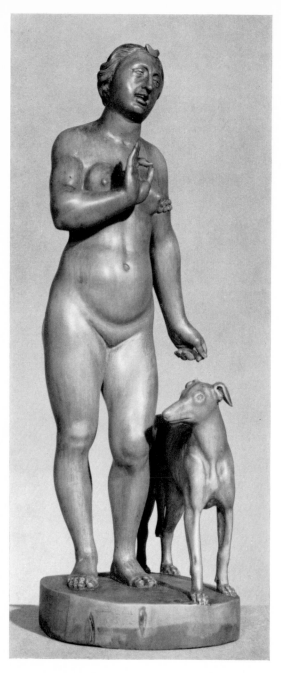

14 LEONARD KERN: Diana (Cat. no. 8)

15 LEONHARD KERN: Diana (Cat. no. 8)

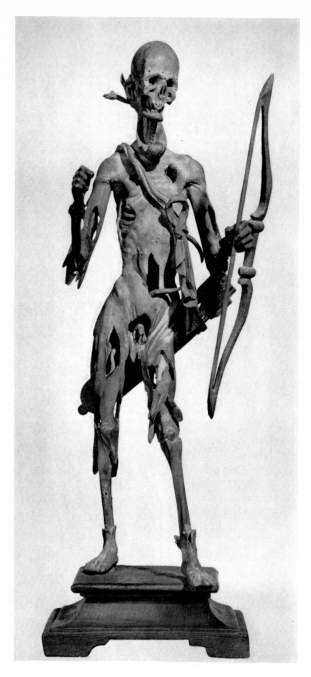

16   BAVARIAN: SECOND HALF OF THE SEVEN-
TEENTH CENTURY: Death (Cat. no. 9)

17 BAVARIAN: SECOND HALF OF THE SEVEN-
TEENTH CENTURY: Death (Cat. no. 9)

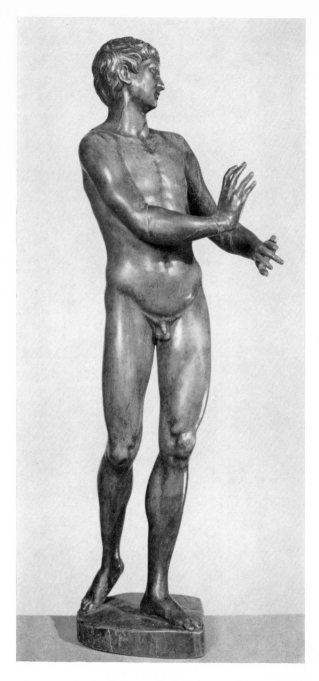

18 SOUTH GERMAN: about 1700: Male Academy
Figure (Cat. no. 10)

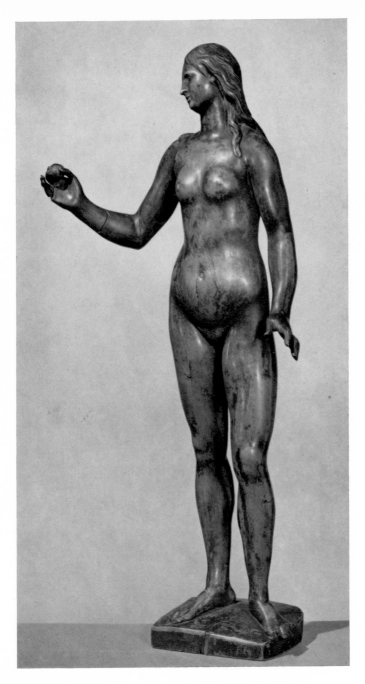

19 SOUTH GERMAN: about 1700: Female Academy
Figure (Cat. no. 10a)

20 AUSTRIAN: FIRST QUARTER OF THE EIGHTEENTH
CENTURY: Courage (Cat. no. 11)

21   AUSTRIAN: FIRST QUARTER OF THE EIGHTEENTH
CENTURY: Fear (Cat. no. 11a)

22 BAVARIAN: EARLY EIGHTEENTH CENTURY:
Alexander (Cat. no. 12)

23   BAVARIAN: EARLY EIGHTEENTH CENTURY:
Julius Caesar (Cat. no. 12a)

24　PAUL EGELL: A Jesuit Saint (Cat. no. 13)

25 PAUL EGELL: A Jesuit Saint (Cat. no. 13)

26   WÜRZBURG: THIRD QUARTER OF THE EIGHTEENTH
CENTURY: A Huntsman (Cat. no. 14)

27 WÜRZBURG: THIRD QUARTER OF THE EIGHTEENTH
CENTURY: A Huntsman (Cat. no. 14)

28 FERDINAND DIETZ: A Goatherd (Cat. no. 15)